It must be for better or worse

For the friends who will remain nameless
Thank you for the stories!

By Gemma Denham

www.gemmadenham.com

Published by Elizabeth Publications
Available from Amazon.com and other retail outlets
Available on Kindle and other devices

Text and illustration copyright © Gemma Denham 2019
Moral rights asserted.

All rights reserved. No part of this publication may be reproduced, stored in a retrieval system, or transmitted, in any form or by any means without prior permission of the author.

ISBN 978-0-9935579-9-6

Contents

Women 12

The Sleeping Beast 14
All Hail 16
Man Flu 18
Toilet troubles 20
Hands that do dishes 22
Lost 24
Shit! 26
One too many 28
Affection 30
Extra time 32
Help 34
Men's Room 36
Void 38
Packhorse 40
Channel Surfing 42
Hell's Kitchen 44
It's a date 46
Hello! 48
I see you baby 50
Cheers! 52
Remote Hog 54
Laundry 56
Mess 58

Remember	....	60
The scenic route	....	62
Ready?	....	64
Score!	....	66
Short but sweet	....	68
Pull my finger	....	70
Eh?	....	72

Men

	....	74
Psychic	....	76
Fine	....	78
Mine	....	80
How do I look?	....	82
Mrs Right	....	84
How Much!	....	86
Hurry up!	....	88
Comfy	....	90
Hidden	....	92
Favourite things	....	94
The Nag	....	96
Running on Empty	....	98
Call the doctor	....	100
Green eyed devil	....	102
The Diet	....	104
The Incredible sulk	....	106
Time	....	108
Shhh!	....	110
Thief	....	112
Pick one!	....	114

Girl talk	....	116
Cheque Please!	....	118
The deadly 5	....	120
Does my bum look big?	....	122
A Moment	....	124
Needy	....	126
Secret weapon	....	128
Faker	....	130
Chatterbox	....	132

Truce

Perfectly Imperfect	....	134

The Sleeping Beast

There is a beast besides me,
Just listen to him roar!
Every sodding breath he takes,
Resulting in a snore.
My body is exhausted.
My eyes oh how they pound.
My head has started aching,
As it's battered by the sound.
How can breathing be so noisy?
How does it not wake him?
By 3am I'm seething,
I could rip him limb from limb!
This has to be abuse,
A form of torture in the least?
To end it would be self-defence,
I'd surely be released?
I just need a female jury.
They would see me in the clear.
I'd leave the courthouse to the sound,
Of applause and cheer.
Then back home to bed I'd rush,
And snuggle myself deep.
And finally I'd get the coveted
Elusive sleep!

All Hail

He entered the room and said
"My dear, I've gone and made the bed".
Forgive me if I hold applause,
And cheer does not escape my jaws,
But as you laid in bed a while
I got through the ironing pile,
I've tidied and I've washed the pots,
I have completed lots and lots
Which I don't announce unto the town,
And so my fella, settle down.
If every task I did got praise
We would be here for days and days.

Man Flu

Everyone stop in your tracks,
Rush round to our house quick!
Please stop what you are doing,
My poor husband is sick.
I'm afraid it is the sniffles
But we're doing all we can.
And yes it could be fatal
Cause you see he is a man.
I had the same cold just last week
Not that you would know.
Because being a female
I did not make a great show.
But pander to him we all must
He's clearly got it worse.
So I've ironed my black dress
And left deposit with the hearse!

Toilet Troubles

If I can lift the lid
And then replace it when I pee.
Why can't he do the same
And leave it nice for me?
On annoyance this rates highly,
It's a bug bear that I hate.
It is most unattractive
To see a toilet in this state.
He's not a training toddler
Who requires it ready, set.
And he knows full well the argument
With which he will be met.
No, he is just a lazy arsed,
None-thinking man.
Please my dear remember
Put the seat down on the can!

Hands That Do Dishes

He'll happily take the dishes out,
I don't even have to ask.
Though he can't ever complete it,
He's half-hearted in his task.
See here's where I am baffled,
I can't work out in my head.
He won't load in the dishwasher
But leave them next to it instead!!
They are *literally* beside it!
Could he annoy me anymore!
I swear he does these things on purpose
Just to laugh at the uproar.
It's not saved anyone anything
The job still needs to be done.
To finish what he's started
Isn't my idea of fun!

LOST

Why can he never find
a single thing about our home?
The countless times he lost his keys and wallet,
Or his phone.
Anything not in his eye line
Might as well just not exist.
It can be right in front of him
Yet still somehow is missed!
He will claim that I have hidden things,
Will claim I've moved his stuff.
He will hustle bustle loudly
Descending deeper in his huff.
I can give exact directions,
I could draw a bloody map.
It won't make one bit of difference
His inner satnav's truly crap!
I've learnt there's just no point in trying
I should get it and be done.
Though sometimes watching him struggle
I'll admit it can be fun!

SHIT!

The lonely, empty loo roll
Has lost its final sheet.
How I wish I'd noticed this
Before I took my seat.
The thought never occurred to me
To check this simple fact.
Now the damage has been done
And I am caught out in the act.
To replace an empty loo roll
Is automatic, is it not?
If he required it on every trip
He would not have forgot.
Now I'm stuck here and I'm stranded
Searching pockets all in vain
For a long forgotten tissue
As I curse his bloody name!

One Too Many

He's trying to be quiet,
He sounds like a buffalo.
As he crashes through the house,
I hear him stumble to and fro.
He's been out with the lads,
He does this every Friday night.
And so it's now the norm to start
Our weekend with a fight.
An awful state as usual,
He's had far too many drinks.
Collapsed in bed besides me
Fucking hell the bastard stinks.
Well enjoy it while you can my dear,
Revenge is mine to take.
With what I've planned for morning
You'll soon realise your mistake!

Affection

He is a sweet and loving man,
I know he shows it when he can,
Or rather (and this is my bane),
When he thinks it will achieve a gain,
To win me round so I'll agree,
- a sneaky move that's so crafty,
When he has desires on the bed,
And thinks with this I will be led.
A kiss, a hug, a gentle pet,
But this is what he doesn't get,
- a woman requires constant love,
Affection comes by far above,
So much in life so don't neglect,
The little things have big effect.
You need to show her that you care,
That it's not just to get in her underwear.

Extra Time

He's brushed his teeth and spat the paste,
And in his hurry, in his haste,
He never takes the time to think,
To wash and rinse around the sink.

There's shaving foam and bits of stubble,
Caught up in every soapy bubble,
The toothpaste tube had lost its cap,
(That man is gonna get a slap!)
And from the middle it's been squeezed,
It's fair to say I am displeased.

The mirror's splashed with God knows what,
My patience and my nerves are shot!
Clean up your mess for pity's sake!
Two extra minutes it would take.
It is a very simple task
And surely not too much to ask!

Help

He is an actual grownup,
A 'partner' in our home.
So why is it I end up
Doing all the chores alone?
It's not the 1950's,
I work and pay my share.
I'm not just 'her indoors'
He should do half it's only fair!
I'm not sure that he sees it,
In the same way that I do.
The mess, the laundry and the pots
Don't show up on his view.
I'm quite sure that without me,
He'd happily live in his own muck.
The mess and the uncleanliness
He wouldn't give a fuck.
And so it's up to me,
As I refuse to live that way.
Have I fallen for a trick?
'More fool me' you'll probably say!

Men's Room

There is a strangeness that occurs
A difference with the 'his' and 'hers'
The amount of time he does consume
In visiting the men's room.
I simply cannot puzzle out
Just what this is all about
He will depart with magazine
And at times I've even seen
Him take his phone – please do not dare
To make a call when you're in there!
We have much nicer rooms for you
To read instead of when you poo
And definitely much more hygienic
It's truly gross I really mean it
And more than just a little crude
Is he that starved of solitude?
In part this practice does offend
Not sure I'll ever comprehend.

VOID

He is void of emotion.
Are all men the same?
It's something I would be keen
To ascertain.
His needs are quite basic,
He lives in 2D,
As a woman it's totally baffling
To me.
I have so many levels,
Emotions galore.
Does he not have them or hide them,
Of this I'm not sure.
He shows hunger and anger,
And horny makes three,
But this is his total
And how can that be?
He must get upset,
Or worried, or scared.
But if he does
It's not something he's shared.
Too much 'manning up',
Too much 'poker face'.
It's as if he's scared
He'll be viewed in disgrace.
But I wish he would open up
Even just for me.
It would bring us closer,
It would set him free.

Packhorse

My fella will scoff
At the size of my bag.
"Look at you carting round
all of your swag."
As into his pockets
His things he will squeeze.
Then turn and ask
"Have you room for my keys?"
He knows what he's doing,
My gaze he evades,
As he follows up shortly with
"Oh and my shades".
Throughout the day,
As I'm sure you have guessed,
Little by little he'll siphon the rest.
I feel like a pack horse,
My shoulder is sore.
I feel I will break
If he adds anymore.
I want to go home,
I'm tired and weary.
My fella tuts loudly,
And then he will query
Why I must always bring so much stuff,
When it so often leaves me out of puff
Is he taking the piss?
I am ready to snap
That cheeky bugger is in for a slap!

Channel Surfing

My eye's started twitching,
I'm feeling quite tense.
If he doesn't choose soon,
He will face consequence.
My fingers are tapping,
I've developed a tick,
On the edge of my seat,
He continues to flick.
I can stand it no longer!
"I beg of you please"
"Just pick one!" I shout
Causing husband to freeze.
He is unaware.
I'm annoyed to my core.
"Just pick one and leave it"
"I can't stand anymore!"
What is the obsession
With every ad break?
Continually flicking
For pity's sake!
Just leave it alone,
It won't kill you to see
The ad's for a minute
SO JUST LET IT BE!

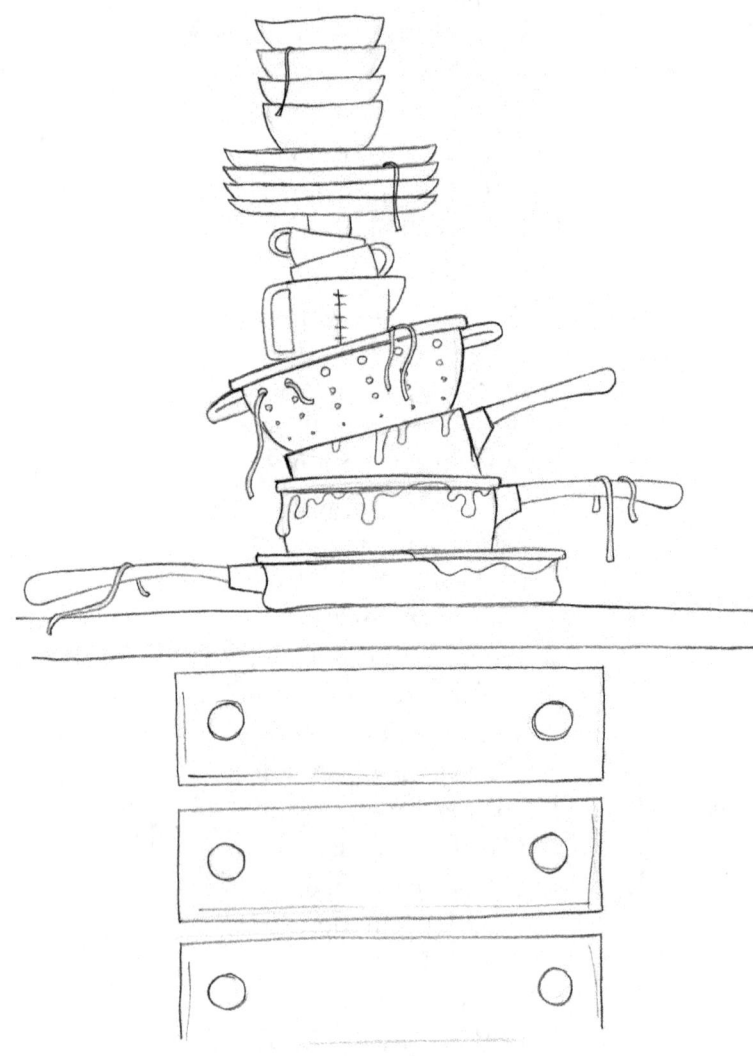

Hell's Kitchen

When he takes unto the kitchen
It is met with some concern.
Don't get me wrong, that boy can cook,
But here's what you must learn.
He cooks with all the flare and grace
Of a possessed mad-man.
So the aftermath's a crime scene
-he uses every single pan!
The kitchen is truly covered
Every surface been explored.
And why in just one meal
Would he need every chopping board?
There is sauce splashed up the walls
Across the floor remnants are strewn.
He's gone through all the forks
Looks like I'm eating with a spoon!
He has cooked though and I'm grateful
I'd pour the wine out but alas
- Unless I want a mug I'll have to go
And wash a glass!

It's a Date!

I have so much to remember,
Stored up in this head of mine.
And really I don't mind it,
For the most part it is fine.

I buy the gifts, I write the cards,
For everyone we know.
Each done with love and care,
And in my choices it will show.

My husband only has the two
Dates important to me.
So don't forget my birthday,
Or our anniversary!

Hello!

It's quite nice in the evenings
To snuggle up and chat.
To take interest in each other
Surely nothing wrong in that?
So why when we're together
Can we never be alone?
I must compete for his attention
As he's always on his phone!
One without the other
I don't think I've ever seen.
If he's not taking a call
He will be looking at the screen.
I wish he'd be here in the moment
With his friends, and me, his wife.
While he's updating his status
He is missing out on life.
Not to mention that this practice is
Incredibly rude.
I feel we need an intervention
So that he can be rescued.
Because although I've tried
It's most important that he knows,
Just how annoying that it is
Before we come to blows!

I SEE YOU BABY

You think I don't notice
You think that you're sly
I see your gaze change
To the corner of your eye
Do you think that she's pretty?
Is she better than me?
You think I don't notice
But baby I see.

She has full perky breasts
So how could you not
There is no denying
She's incredibly hot
But I am your girl
So all eyes on me
You think I don't notice
But baby I see.

Cheers!

Oh how my heart sinks
When from carton he drinks
It is dirty and vile
And it's quite infantile
Can he not comprehend
That the image he sends
Is of cheap, nasty scum
That's not what we've become
And does he really think
Someone else will take drink
Now it's covered in spit
He's a lazy half-wit
Please have a bit of class
And go and find a glass!

Remote Hog

The King of his castle
He sits on his throne
He rules over the TV
And the programmes that are shown
The sceptre he holds
Well, that is the remote
And he wields it with power
His face set in a gloat
Enjoy the brief victory
You've got your own way
Tomorrow I'll be quicker
And you'll watch what I say!

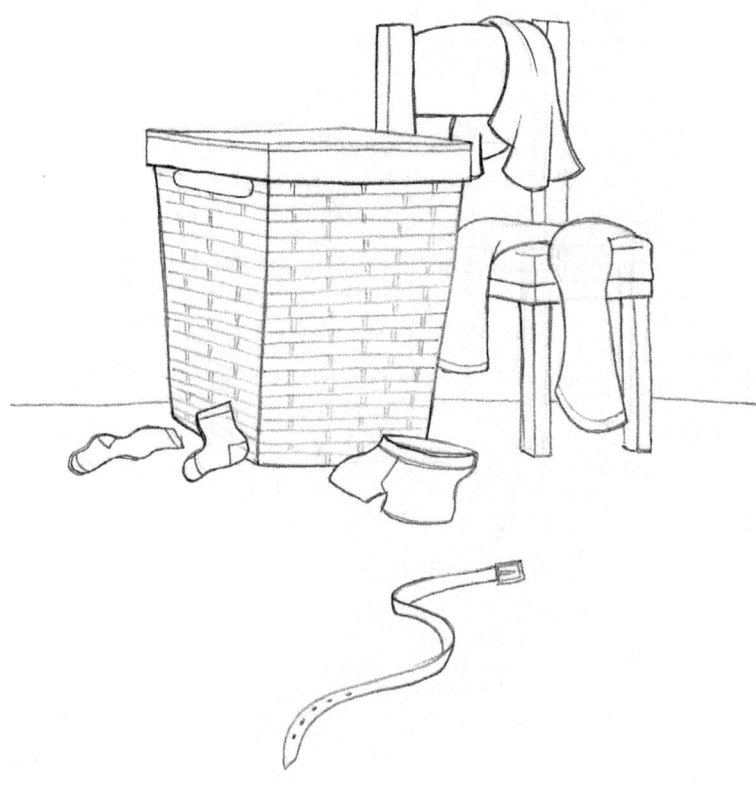

Laundry

It's oh so close,
But just not quite.
The pile of laundry's still in sight.

Next to the basket,
Not quite there.
Or hung and slung about a chair.

Kicked to the corner
Of the floor
His secret stash behind the door.

It's surely not that hard for him,
To lift the lid and drop it in.

My frustration I just cannot mask it
Use the bloody laundry basket!

Mess

Am I the only one that sees the mess?
He'll never tidy up unless
I've asked him several times or more
Otherwise he can ignore
I'd really, really like to know
How does it not annoy him so?
Does he just wait until I crack?
And tidy up, and put things back
All he must do is wait it out
Put up with the occasional shout
I really wish he'd do his bit
The bone idle, lazy git!

Remember

He forgets to take his wallet,
He forgets to take his phone.
He forgets what he was buying,
Cause he left the list at home.
He forgets to post the letter,
Though he holds it in his hand.
I swear that man is living in
His own cloud cuckoo land!
He forgets when we are meeting,
He forgets to phone his mum.
Is he really that forgetful?
Or does the bugger just play dumb?
Does he even listen?
Is his mind really a sieve?
At the start it was amusing
Now it's harder to forgive.
My assumptions have concluded
In reality he can
Remember when he wants
The problems his attention span!

The Scenic Route

"We're not lost it's the scenic way"
He says to keep my fears at bay
But there is no fooling me
We are as lost, as lost can be
But being a pig-headed man
He'll keep going as far as he can
He'll not admit he does not know
Won't claim defeat, let weakness show
Won't stop to ask a passer-by
And so he'll continue the lie
That this is the route he meant to take
Heaven forbid he admits mistake
He of course can do no wrong
Which is why our journey's twice as long!

Ready?

I take my time with my outfit,
And choosing what to wear.
Also with hair and make-up,
Each one is done with care.

My husband on the other hand,
(Still wearing last night's shirt)
Looks like I've dragged him from a ditch,
He's so covered in dirt!

He'll not even take the time
To shave before we go.
I feel I'm catwalk ready
While he looks like a hobo.

He reckons he looks 'rugged'
More like he's a lazy bum.
He made the effort while we dated
Just what has he become?

What other people think of us
Lord only knows!
The least you could do my dear
Is put on some clean clothes!

Score!

All my shows have disappeared,
They have cancelled them all.
And in their place they've only gone
And put sodding football!
As if that wasn't bad enough
My husband is a fan.
He once tried to get me interested
That's where the fight began.
I tried hard to watch the match
I tried with all my might.
I left before halftime
That game is really fucking shite!
And now it's on for weeks
Our TV blasts out every match.
While my husband sits there drinking beer
And having a good scratch.

Short but sweet?

I send a message from the heart
Pour out my soul to him.
The message I get in reply's
Always a little thin.

*"I hope your day is going well
And thank you for last night.
It was just what I needed
You are truly a delight.
I wish I'd met you sooner
You mean the world to me.
I love you so, so much
I feel as lucky as can be xxx"*

Some advice for all you men
I'll give a little clue.
The correct response to text like that
Is never "Yeah, me too"!

Pull My Finger

I'm of the realisation
Men are simply just tall boys.
It can be quite endearing
But in part it just annoys.

Never more apparent
That the child within does linger.
Is when he turns to me with grin
And tells me 'pull my finger'.

He thinks this is hilarious,
I'm totally repulsed!
Tears are streaming down his face
And in his laughter he's convulsed.

Another of his party tricks,
(the vile, disgusting twerp)
Is how he likes to make
A song and dance of every burp!

Each one is a performance,
He cares not of who might hear.
I cringe at what the neighbours think
It is a real fear.

EH?

It goes in one ear
And straight out the other.
Leaving me standing here
Feeling like your mother!
Why can't you bloody listen?
It's just common decency.
Nodding and agreeing
Really isn't fooling me!
I think you need to try again,
Have another go.
Think you're being smart?
The answer wasn't 'yes' or 'no'!

Psychic

I'm not a mind reader,
Give me a bloody clue.
Is it something that I've done?
Or something I'm supposed to do?
I saw the mood transcend you,
I pray to God it won't last long.
I'm walking round on eggshells
Trying to think where I've gone wrong.
Can you not just tell me?
Instead you watch me stew.
I'd apologise for what I'd done,
If I only bloody knew.
Your subtle hints are useless.
So I'll save us all some time.
I'm sorry and I love you,
Have some chocolate and some wine!

Fine

I'm by no means an expert,
But I'm put on high alert,
It is cause to disconcert,
Cause she tells me she is *'fine'*.

I just don't know what is best,
Intervene or let her rest,
She needs to get it off her chest,
But she tells me she is *'fine'*.

Someone say how to begin,
There's no way that I can win,
What if I offer her some Gin?
Please send help! She says she's *'fine'*!

Mine

You ordered the salad,
And that was just fine.
So eyes off my plate,
These chips are all mine.
If you wanted some,
You should have ordered some too.
Don't you dare do,
What I know you will do.
A sweet smile won't cut it,
Neither will sweet talk.
If your hand comes on over,
I'll stab it with my fork!
You live with your choice,
The options were there.
I ordered the chips,
So they're mine,
NOT to share!

How do I look?

When you hold your clothes up for me,
And ask as breezy as can be,
For me to choose which one looks best
I'm just wishing you would get dressed.
Do you really think I care
Which outfit you decide to wear?
Because I don't even a bit,
My dear I do not give a shit.
It does not matter anyway,
You will not choose the one I say,
Whichever one you will look great,
So hurry up, it's getting late.

Mrs Right

Why must she always win the fight?
Why's she the one who's always right?
She has to have the final say,
I'm not allowed to get my way.
This may seem a surprise to you,
But my opinion matters too!
I am not always in the wrong,
My argument is just as strong.
But facts and figures soon get misted,
Soon my argument gets twisted,
And she's coming out on top,
There's no way I can make it stop!
A car crash right before my eyes,
A witness to my own demise,
She is the victor, head held high,
The defeat hurts, I will not lie.
I was convinced that I was right,
But she will always win the fight.

HOW MUCH!

I was feeling cheerful,
Till along came the post.
Amongst them the one,
I always dread the most.
Now I'm shocked to my core,
And I'm feeling quite ill
As with shaking hands,
I look down at the bill.
She's done it again!
I will kill her I swear!
As I recognise payments,
For clothes, shoes and hair.
Her wardrobe is bursting,
She does not need more.
It's stacked to the rafters,
It's in every drawer.
I must get her card,
It has to be chopped.
It's the only way,
That she will be stopped!
I can't take anymore,
She drives me to despair,
It's for the good of our marriage,
It's because I care.
I love her but my God she needs reining in.
Her spending is manic,
My patience worn thin.

Hurry Up!

Jesus! How long does one person need?
Time is a 'ticking,
Let's pick up the speed!
We told them that we would be there by 9.
Just put on the black one,
Yes those shoes look fine.
All I require is shit, shave and shower.
I'm ready to go all within half an hour.
My missis by contrast,
Will take half a day!
She does so much prepping,
I stay out of the way.
The bathroom is steamed up,
There's perfume galore,
Her whole shoe collection,
Will scatter the floor.
Outfit upon outfit discarded in piles,
While she picks and dismisses the various styles.
I've learnt not to moan.
Through my teeth I will smile.
Whilst constantly checking my watch all the while.

Comfy?

What is with all of these cushions and throws?
Adorning the bed
And the sofa in droves.
So many there's barely enough room to sit.
I feel I must perch on the edge
Just to fit.
They may look inviting,
But comfy they're not.
To snuggle in I have to remove the lot!
And what is the point
Of them upon our bed?
They serve no actual purpose
Have you lost your head?
No-one else sees them,
Except you and I.
Each night we must clear them,
Before we can lie.
This only achieves to create a new chore.
And we've plenty of those,
Please don't make any more!

Hidden

One minute they're there,
And the next they are gone.
Something keeps happening,
Something is wrong.
If I put it down,
Then that's where it should stay.
Stop moving my things,
Stop tidying them away!
It's so damn infuriating,
Why can't you see?
They are my possessions,
So leave it to me.
Then I could find things,
Not be at a loss.
And you wouldn't moan,
You would never get cross.
So you deal with your things,
And I'll deal with mine.
That way we're more likely
To get along fine.

Favourite things

She's got dresses and trousers,
And shirts, skirts and jackets.
Boots, heels and trainers,
And tights all in packets.
Necklaces, bracelets
And so many rings.
These are a few of her favourite things.

Make-up in all colours,
So she never clashes.
Packs of fake nails,
And some of eyelashes.
Eyeliner pencils to draw
On her 'wings'
These are a few of her favourite things.

Bursting wardrobe.
Overflowing.
Leaves me feeling sad.
This woman has so much of everything,
It makes me feel so mad.

The Nag

Stop nagging woman,
I'll put the pots away.
They don't need immediate response,
They'll last another day.

Stop nagging woman,
The windows I will clean.
They're really not that bad,
Stop saying that they're going green!

Stop nagging woman,
I will take out the trash.
But first I have to meet the lads,
They're in town on the lash.

You nag me in the mornings.
You nag me noon and night.
A constant buzz upon my ear
Looking for a fight.

I've put it on my job list.
The process has begun.
I don't need constant reminder,
Just trust it will be done.

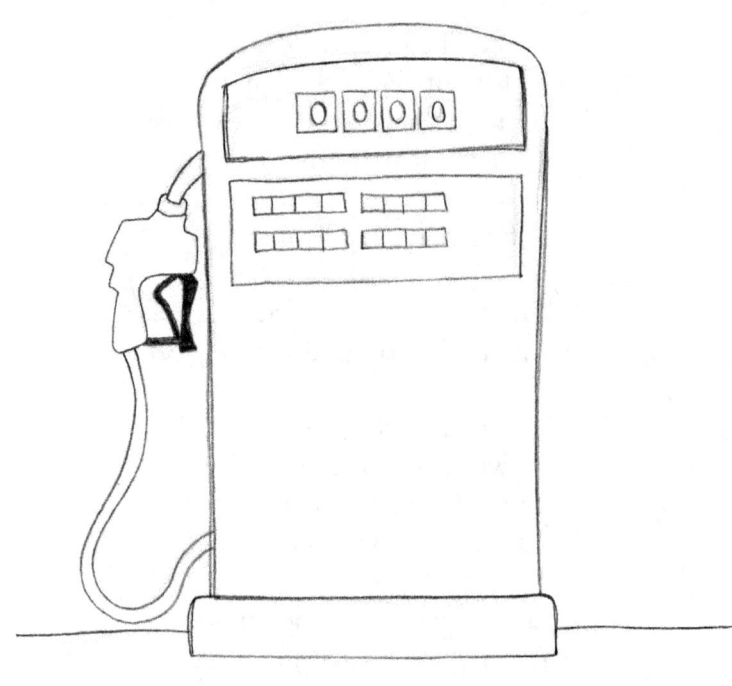

Running on Empty

What is the aversion
To filling up the car?
You do know without petrol
That it won't go very far?
Entering your car is always done
With a sense of dread.
I just know the little needle
Will be pointing in the red!
Please, I beg, just fill it up
When it starts getting low.
It's not good for the car
And you know it annoys me so.
If you run it to the ground
I will not come to your rescue.
It's completely avoidable
So the fault will lie with you.
And whilst you sit beside the road
Waiting on a tow.
Just picture me home laughing
Shouting that I told you so!

Call the Doctor

My arms ache to hold you,
I need to feel your touch.
We've not lain together for so long,
I need you so damn much.
It's not like when we were dating,
Back then we were so wired.
But now you've had a long day,
And you tell me you are tired.
Or the other favourite
Excuse you like to make.
"Not tonight my darling
I have this awful headache"
We need to call a doctor.
This surely can't be right.
To have this many headaches
And be so tired every night.
I'm feeling quite rejected.
I'm feeling quite forlorn.
Oh well, at least I kept hold of
My secret stash of porn!

Green Eyed Devil

Why is she so suspicious
That she wants to read my text,
And tries to eavesdrop on my phone calls,
For fuck's sake what is next?

Why is she so suspicious
I can't have a female friend,
Without it causing a commotion,
When is this gonna end?

Why is she so suspicious
That she must always tag along,
To my each and every outing,
I just don't know what is wrong!

In part it is a little cute,
I know it shows you care.
But it's only going to form a wedge
And drive me to despair!

You are the only girl I want
You mean the world to me
But you're gonna have to calm it down
For Christ's sake let me be!

The Diet

Oh God she's on a diet.
She's cutting this and that.
Reducing her carb intake,
Banning all sugar and fat.
We're all in for a bumpy ride,
Buckle up and hold on tight!
Maybe if I keep my distance
Then this will turn out alright.
It's great she wants to lose some weight,
Improve the way she looks.
I have no problem with the concept
Only in the way she cooks.
You see, if she can't have it
It would appear neither can I.
This is most unacceptable
I'm still a growing guy!
I'm not on a diet –
I didn't sign up to this shit!
I'm happy with the way I look
Why must I take a bloody hit!
Well I will eat the salad,
And I'll eat it with a smile.
Then when she goes to bed
I'll stuff my face a good long while!

The Incredible Sulk

I've done something wrong,
I've stepped out of line.
She's suddenly quiet,
She says she is *'fine'*.
Her face says differently,
It's subtle but there.
The frown and the pout,
The anger in her glare.
Silent treatment for me,
As my punishment.
For as long as it takes,
For me to repent.
The problem with this
What she doesn't know
I quite like the quiet,
I enjoy it so.
And so my sweet angel,
Take as long as you need,
The sorry you're looking for
Won't come at speed.
It's quite a nice break
For the chatter to cease.
I mean no offence,
But I welcome the peace!

Time

I should have known from our first date,
When she turned up an hour late,
That she could never be on time,
At first I thought this would be fine.
I found it funny, found it cute,
But this is now in dispute,
And cause of many a feud,
Because, frankly, I find it rude!
It's surely not that difficult
(I mean, she is a grown adult!)
To be ready and get there
On time, come on it's only fair,
And what makes me really mad,
Is I appear equally bad!
So in our plans I always lie,
Add a time buffer to get us by,
That way I'm given fighting chance,
To not be last through the entrance.

Shhh!

If there were awards for talking
My missis would win the gold!
She will barely pause for breath
It's really something to behold.
She can even answer for you
No she will not hold her tongue.
Cause if you were to answer for yourself
You'd surely answer wrong!
The topic is no matter
She's an opinion on them all.
And if you dare to disagree
Well then you're looking for a fall!
I've learnt to come to peace with it
I'll sit and nod and smile.
And interject with a "Yes dear"
Every once in a while.

Thief

Her wardrobe's bursting at the seams
So why must she revert
To going through my drawers to find
And steal my t-shirt?

This is done without consulting me
Her riffling through my stack.
And if I want it I'm expected
To ask *her* for the bugger back!

How did things get so twisted?
It is mine for me to wear.
At what point did our clothes become
Something for us to share?

Pick One!

Do not give her options.
Do not give her a choice.
It is the only time I've found
That she will lose her voice.

She's unable to pick quickly.
Great thought she'll have to give,
And still she'll struggle with a choice
She's so indecisive!

I know she has an opinion,
I hear it every day.
So why is it so difficult to
Just pick one and say!

Girl Talk

What goes on in our bedroom,
Should stay between the sheets.
It's not topic for conversation,
When you and your friend meet.

Some things should remain private.
Keep them guarded for all they're worth.
I shouldn't have to fear them knowing
About length and girth!

I'm sure you wouldn't like it,
If I did the same to you.
And you had to meet up with my mates,
Knowing that they all knew.

It makes me quite uncomfortable.
I am a private guy.
When bumping into friends
I cannot look them in the eye.

I see the smiles and whispers.
Don't think that I don't know.
I hope at least you're being kind
I've a delicate ego!

Cheque Please!

Wherever we may go,
Out for a drink or to a show,
The expectation seems to be,
That the bill should come to me.

Well sorry to sound a jerk,
But we both go out to work,
And so in this modern day,
Why am I the one who has to pay?

Surely it's only fair,
If the paying out we share.
It's not the 50's anymore,
Equal rights have won the war.
So let's stop living in the past,
And give this thing a blast,
And sorry to burst your bubble
- But it's your round and mine's a double!

The Deadly 5
(Definition of terms used by women)

'Go ahead' is not permission
It's a dare, abort the mission!
Do not do it, run away
Or she will surely make you pay.

'Whatever' is code for 'fuck you'
So what I recommend you do
Apologise and do it fast
Keep your head down till the storm's passed.

'Nothing' is red alarm
It's something and could cause you harm
You need to find out what you've done
And take restorative action!

'Fine' can be deadliest of all
You're in for an almighty fall
You're in the wrong, you've been a dick
Apologise and do it quick.

'Wow' is not a compliment
You've cocked up big, you should repent
It's said in shock that you're that dumb
Best to play dead, this one's fearsome!

Does my bum look big?

Does my bum look big in this?
My dear, are you taking the piss?
There's not one answer I could give
To convince it's not massive.
If I look up and say no,
Well then I've answered far too slow.
If I comment on your beauty,
I'm distracting from your booty.
If I dared to tell you 'yes'
You can imagine the distress
And the anger that would rein,
So from this I shall refrain.
Can we stop this silly farce?
I think you have a lovely arse.
So can we please just leave it there?
It is the truth my dear I swear.

A Moment

I cannot take a moment,
To sit just peacefully,
To get lost in a daydream,
Let everything just be.

I cannot sit in silence,
At least I can't for long.
She'll ask me what I'm thinking,
She'll ask me what is wrong.

Sometimes a guy just likes to sit,
And at those times you'll find,
That there is nothing bothering him,
And nothing on his mind.

It is the truth I swear it.
I do not wear a mask.
At least everything was just fine,
Till you started to ask!

Needy

I took too long to reply,
She took offence, I made her cry,
I put two kisses and not three,
Now she's suspicious of me.
I find I must go out my way,
To call and compliment all day,
We must cuddle, must hold hands,
These are but few of her demands.
It's nice and mostly I don't mind,
But every so often I will find,
It feels the walls are closing in,
Claustrophobia begins.
So please allow a little grace,
Sometimes it's nice to have some space.

Secret Weapon

My missis, she plays dirty.
The fight is never fair.
If she begins to lose,
Well then you had better beware.
She has a secret weapon,
Just waiting on her call.
To stop you in your tracks,
She'll let the tears start to fall.
It is a devious move,
She is master at her game.
As how can I continue,
When the poor girl looks so lame.
I know it's a production.
I know it's all for show.
But when she starts to cry
I lose all my bravado!
We'll kiss and have a cuddle.
She's won and feeling smug.
I could kick myself for caving,
What a complete and utter mug.

Faker

My girl's a natural beauty,
Not that you'd ever know.
She hides beneath her make-up,
Puts on some other show.
She'll dose herself in fake tan,
To colour up her skin,
Her eyebrows are highly defined,
The buggers are coloured in!
Her lips are always colourful,
With red and deep plum splashes,
Her eyes heavily laden,
By the weight of her fake lashes.
Her hair made from extensions,
The curls they fall in trails.
Another glued on bit of course
-her long manicured nails.
She feels ugly without all this,
To me she looks divine.
I wish she'd leave the fake behind
And let her beauty shine.

Chatterbox

Movie, drama or a match
When watching TV there's a catch,
The type of programme doesn't matter
My girl will constantly chatter!
It makes no difference what I do,
Her words will continue to spew,
I've tried to 'shush' it doesn't work,
It only makes her go berserk.
My problem with this won't compute,
I wish she came with pause or mute,
Instead I must stay strong, withstand,
And be thankful for on demand!

Perfectly Imperfect

At times you do annoy me,
I really can't deny.
And all your little nuances,
Can leave me asking why?
But when I look upon your face,
And gaze into your eyes.
The feelings that I'm met with,
Come as no great surprise.
Yes we have our differences,
But that's what makes you you.
I wouldn't change you for the world,
I swear my dear it's true.
I love you with my very soul,
We really do connect.
You are the only one for me,
So perfectly imperfect.

WITH THANKS

A huge thank you to all of my friends who
knowingly or not contributed to this book.
For your own protection you shall remain nameless.

Thank you to my two proof readers
the wonderful Gary Parker and Carol Page.

A big thank you to the lovely Rebecca Slorach,
my fantastic editor, and fabulous friend.
Your help as always has been priceless,
and I cannot thank you enough.

And lastly, thank you to my
wonderful partner for his love and support
and for not doing the majority of
things mentioned in this book.
Hopefully I don't either!

Others in the series....

There are also many other books by Gemma
check out her website:

WWW.GEMMADENHAM.COM

for more information, or follow her
@gemmaEdenham   gemmadenhamauthorillustrator

www.ingramcontent.com/pod-product-compliance
Lightning Source LLC
Chambersburg PA
CBHW070430010526
44118CB00014B/1984